Overcoming
Fear and Worry

H. NORMAN WRIGHT

AspirePress

Torrance, California

AspirePress

Overcoming Fear and Worry
Copyright © 2014 H. Norman Wright
All rights reserved.
Aspire Press, an imprint of Rose Publishing, Inc.
4733 Torrance Blvd., #259
Torrance, California 90503 USA
www.aspirepress.com

Printed in the United States of America
020215RRD

Contents

CHAPTER ONE

Fear

I t's an intruder. It's also an interference with everyday life. It can come and go at will and take the edge off of life. You've heard of a joy robber—well, this is it. At times there's a good reason for its presence, and then there are times when having it around doesn't make sense. What is this? Fear. It has the power to either immobilize or motivate, but in either case, it can cast a cloud over what may have been a positive experience.[1]

We all experience fear to one degree or another. It can range from the smallest fear of not looking good enough to the concern of not getting home safely from school each day. Some of us talk about our fear, while others just live with its presence and remain silent about it.

While it's true that many feel secure today, that feeling could be a sense of false security. I have met with many in schools and companies who seem so secure but inwardly live with fear. I have sat with survivors of 9/11, Hurricane Katrina, school shootings, and accidents, as well as those who seemingly lead everyday secure lives. I hear about fear, and the security we seem to experience can disappear in the blink of an eye.

For many, the illusion of security that was lived with for so long has dissolved. Millions of Americans—as well as people in other countries—who never before experienced fear and panic now do.

Over the past decade, we have become more safety conscious. Many people used to let their kids run around the neighborhood, but now worries about stranger danger have made us more cautious. Many parents bring their children to school instead of sending them on the school bus; airports and places of business have increased security; and Coast Guard and Navy boats patrol our harbors and coasts.

The media pours frightening stories into our homes twenty-four hours a day, further eroding our feeling of safety. Just watch the news each night. It will intensify your fear!

You can find freedom from the grip of fear.

We're the richest nation on earth. We've always found security in our savings, stocks, mutual funds, retirement, and so on. Until recently. Lately, major corporations have failed, pension plans have been drained, and the stock market has been erratic—these situations too feed our fear on a daily basis.

Each day I talk with people whose lives are filled with fear. Some of them have recently developed fears; others have lived in a prison of fear since childhood. The good news is that the prison doors of fear are unlocked! Remember, no matter how long you have been imprisoned behind its bars, you can find freedom from the grip of fear and walk away from it.

What Is Fear?

Our English word *fear* comes from the Old English *faer*, meaning "sudden calamity or danger." Fear has come to mean the emotional response to real or imagined danger.

The Hebrew word for fear can also be translated *dread*, meaning a heavy, oppressive sensation of fear.

A word we often interchange with fear is *anxiety*, which comes from the Latin *anxius*. To be anxious is to be troubled in mind about some uncertain event. A variation of *anxius* means "to press tightly or to strangle." Anxiety is often a suffocating experience. Fear and anxiety are actually quite similar. A true fear has an identifiable object of danger, either real (a burglar in your house) or imagined (a shadow that looks like a burglar). When we're anxious, we have the same feeling of fear, but we don't know why.

We show our fear in different ways. Some people experience a sensation internally and show nothing on the outside. Others sweat, and their heart pounds. Some people become unglued, start screaming, and run away. Others freeze and cannot move. Habakkuk the prophet experienced some of the common effects of fear:

> *"I heard, and my [whole inner self] trembled, my lips quivered at the sound. Rottenness enters into my bones and under me [down to my feet]; I tremble."*
>
> — Habakkuk 3:16, AMP

Also, the skin can appear pale, hair stand on end, and blood pressure rise. There may be increased blood flowing through the muscles, causing greater tension; dryness and tightness of the throat and mouth; an increased need to urinate and defecate; butterflies flying in your stomach; a paralyzing weakness in the arms and legs; difficulty in breathing or a tightness in the chest. Scripture gives the same description of the results of fear and worry:

> *"Anxiety in a man's heart weighs it down."*
>
> — Proverbs 12:25, AMP

Rational and Irrational Fears

Fear of Life

All of us are afraid sometimes. That's normal. But some of us are fearful most of the time. That's *not* normal. We weren't designed to be driven by fear, yet some of us are. We weren't created to dread life, yet many of us do.

Occasionally, people tell me that they are afraid of death. That's not unusual, but even more people I talk to are afraid of life in one way or another. Living life to its full potential is a threat to them. They're emotionally paralyzed and refuse to participate in many of life's normal experiences. They hide and insulate themselves and throw away their opportunity to live life. When counseling them, I often say, "It seems you're immobilized by fear," and they agree!

> **We weren't designed to be driven by fear.**

There's a difference between being afraid and being immobilized by fear. We may be afraid at times, but we're not to live our lives in fear. Paul wrote:

"For the Spirit God gave us does not make us timid [fearful], but gives us power, love and self-discipline."

— 2 Timothy 1:7

Isn't it strange for us to choose to imprison ourselves in fear, especially when Christ came to set us free?

The fear of life is actually more debilitating than the fear of death. Fear disables. Fear shortens life. Fear cripples our relationships with others. Fear blocks our relationship with God. Fear makes life a chore. We become the living dead. In the words of John Haggai, a leader in ways to overcome tough situations:

Having a fear is like having a cancer. It is always there, hidden inside you, always sapping your strength and breaking your concentration. Even rational fear can be destructive in its effects.

You cannot hide fear. Its destruction begins by feeding on you, and then moving into your social and physical environment.[2]

The fear of life is the fear of being hurt, being rejected, making a mistake, showing imperfections, and failing as a person. Fearing rejection is a common response for all of us as we grow up, but it becomes destructive when it continues and weaves its way into our adulthood. Somewhere along our path in life, we may subconsciously decide not to be vulnerable and never to take a risk. Before long we become turtles tucked inside a defensive shell of fear, immobile and detached from life. Like turtles, we'll only progress in life when we stick our necks out.

Exaggerated Fear

One day a friend and I were fishing at a mountain lake. We were working on a nice string of fish when it started to rain, and in just a few minutes the shower became a downpour. We hated to leave our fishing spot, but we decided that dry was better than wet. So we climbed into my friend's car and drove up the mountain road.

As we ascended to a higher elevation, the rain turned to snow, and soon the snowstorm was heavy and intense. When we crested a slight hill, the car began an uncontrollable spin on the slippery road. I realized we were sliding helplessly toward a roadside cliff, so I reached to unbuckle my seat belt in order to jump out before the car slid over the edge. However, in a few seconds the car did a complete 360 and came to a stop in the middle of the road.

> Normal fear reacts, but exaggerated fear overreacts.

The life-threatening danger was over, but my friend and I had been plunged into a state of fear. There was nothing we could do about the way our bodies reacted; we had accelerated heart rates, a sinking feeling in our stomachs, and white, blood-drained skin. We stayed on edge emotionally as we crept down the hill into town, briefly losing control of the car on two curves.

Our experience on the slick road illustrates a legitimate and rational fear: We could have lost our lives. But many who are plagued by irrational fear would end up exaggerating the danger of our close call and swear never again to go fishing, drive on a mountain road, or drive in the snow. An exaggerated fear is equipped with binoculars; it tends to magnify dangers that are a great distance away, making small threats appear large.

Normal fear reacts, but exaggerated fear overreacts. In many areas of the country, there seems to be larger-than-normal amount of danger and violence—freeway shootings, gang wars, kidnappings, and so forth. Most people react normally to these dangers by being cautious on freeways and avoiding some potentially dangerous areas of the city. But those with exaggerated fear overreact by confining themselves to their homes or neighborhoods.

Fear of Fear

Some people actually fear the sensation of fear itself, so they go out of their way to avoid all places and situations that produce these sensations. Since they cannot avoid the involuntary knot in the stomach or the white (or sometimes flushed) complexion that accompanies a frightening experience, they avoid any setting in which these feelings might possibly occur. For example, someone who is afraid of loud and dominant individuals may overcompensate by avoiding meeting new people altogether.

Fear of Thoughts

Some people may not be afraid of their feelings but are afraid of their thoughts. Have you ever wished that a frightening thought would go away—or would never have entered your mind in the first place? *I'm going to forget the host's name, or I won't remember the opening lines of my presentation.* Occasional thoughts like these are normal and relatively harmless, but the persistent fear of these thoughts is abnormal.

COMMON FEARS IN DAILY LIFE

What part does fear play in your life? Let's consider daily life. Fears covers the gamut of human experience and includes fear of exams, spiders, darkness, mice, heights, and rejection—among hundreds of other things.

There are healthy and unhealthy fears. But do you know the difference? Healthy fears may prompt you to:

➢ Wear a seat belt in a plane or car to avoid injury.

➢ Wear a life jacket in a canoe on a river trip.

➢ Check with an expert before eating wild mushrooms.

➢ Ask a financial expert for advice before making investments.

Any of these normal concerns and fears could move into the unhealthy stage by never riding in a car, plane or canoe; never eating any mushrooms; never investing. Severe anxiety or fear hinders a person's performance. It can actually cause paralysis.

But what about the benefits of fear or anxiety? Many individuals in various professions have said that a mild degree of fear and anxiety increases their effectiveness. Actors, speakers, politicians, football players, salespeople, runners, and fighter pilots are a few of those individuals who feel they perform better with a certain amount of anxiety.

In an extreme crisis, however, fear may be so intense that the panic creates even greater trauma. A person running from a fire in a restaurant may run into the street without looking and be struck by a car. Too much fear brings mistakes. But too little fear can cause carelessness and even a disregard for dangerous situations. Firefighters can't be rash and careless, nor can army troops.

We were not created to live in a continual state of apprehension. Our lives are not to be a reflection of timidity and fear. You may want deliverance from fear, but you should not want deliverance from all of your fears. Fear is the fuel that moves you out of a dangerous situation. Positive fear can save your life. It is fear that gnaws at your life and disrupts your sense of calmness that we seek to eliminate.

Much of our fear is directed toward possible eventualities, and here is where our fear changes into worry. A heart attack, the stock market collapsing, another world war, and the end of the world are all things that cannot be prevented by fearing them. The energy that we expend in fear and worry can keep us in a state of anxiety as it builds and swells within us. We end up being too afraid to live life!

What do you fear most—falling off a thousand-foot cliff? Being attacked and gored by a raging bull? Probably not. Unusual situations like these are not usually what frighten us. It is more the everyday events and people who threaten us to such an extent that our life is limited.

Whatever it is that you fear most, do you think you're the only one who feels that way? Think about yourself as you read about three common fears.

1. *Fear of rejection.* Rejection is feeling unaccepted by yourself, other people, or both. Somewhere in your lifetime you may have been treated like an unacceptable person. Someone, even a parent, may have seen you as a burden. If you were rejected as a child, you may either retreat from others or, out of your fear of rejection, seek approval so intense that you push others away.

Many people are afraid of socializing with others, especially strangers. They might be able to perform great feats and acts of courage, but they cringe when it comes to reaching out to people. Their fear of others cries out until other people become aware of their discomfort. Other people may just decide to leave such intense people alone, and then the discomforting people are left with the feeling of being rejected. Fear of reaching out to others and fear of being rejected go hand in hand.

Another way to experience rejection (and loneliness) is to avoid socializing and become a recluse. You may feel a desperate need for affection and approval, but when love is offered, you reject it because you question its sincerity. A rejected person short-circuits any acceptance that is offered to him or her. Thus the fear the rejected person feels intensifies.

Fear is like that—it involves two kinds of pain. One kind is the pain of experiencing the situation, and the other kind comes from avoiding what you are afraid of. Either way the pain exists. What most of us do not realize, however, is that in the long run, the pain of doing something we're afraid of is less than the pain of avoiding it.

2. *Fear of failure.* Fearful people are often perfectionists. Their security comes from doing things better than anyone else. They either drive themselves and others up a wall in their quest for perfection or they listen to their fear and retreat. They fear ridicule from others and their own inner voices when they are not perfect.

If you're a perfectionist, you expend more effort than others yet feel no real satisfaction. In a sense you are a successful failure, continually striving to do better. You are never satisfied with yourself or others. Interruptions, disruptions, changes, irregularities, delays, and surprises are your enemies. Your theme song is strive, strive, strive— an endless treadmill.

There are times, though, when a perfectionist deals with his or her fear by retreating rather than striving. This perfectionist withdraws and hesitates, because the pain of failure is too much. By not trying, he or she can always think, *I can do it if I try, or I know I could really do it if I wanted to . . . or had the time.* But if he or she tries, that hope would be lost. Withdrawal becomes a protective cocoon.

The unreasonable demands of perfectionists placate their need to please themselves or others or to feel adequate and eliminate the fear of failure. But whatever is driving them has an insatiable appetite.

If you're a perfectionist, what or who are you afraid of? We can never achieve perfection in this life. We can become confident and, based on this confidence, do the best we can. Our confidence comes from a declaration from God Himself who has declared us to be adequate people. He did this through His Son, Jesus, and His work on the cross. Think about it.

3. *Fear of people.* One of the most common problems of life is the fact that one of our greatest fears is the fear of people. Imagine one person fearing another person—people fearing people. This fear comes in various shapes and sizes: and inferiority, shyness, and timidity all reflect this fear. Sometimes these fears become extreme and move into agoraphobia—the fear of being in public.[3]

The Causes and Effects of Fear

How do our fears develop? They grow out of experiences or situations in our childhood. They may have been modeled for us by our parents, and in some ways we pattern our life after them. In many cases our childhood interactions with significant people form our response to others and to ourselves.

How much of what you do is motivated by fear? Do you know? Have you ever thought about how your life may be dominated by fear? Think about these statements and see if they apply to your own life:

> ➢ Fear of what others think about us keeps us from being friendly or speaking up in class.

> ➢ Fear of others getting more than us or a better position causes us to act impulsively, to try to beat others, or to devalue others by gossip.

> ➢ Fear of being controlled by others or of having to conform causes us to dominate others.

➢ Fear of sharing our weaknesses and inadequacies causes us to act like the strong silent type.

➢ Fear of failure keeps us in a life of mediocrity and boredom.

➢ Fear of financial ruin keeps us from wise investments and/or makes us dull and boring by our careful restrictive lifestyle.

➢ Fear of God makes us distort who he really is.

And the fears go on and on. What is your fear? What does it cause you to do?

_____

_____

_____

_____

_____

_____

_____

Two Great Motivators—Hope and Fear

There are two great motivating forces in life: fear and hope. Interestingly, both of these motivators can produce the same result.

Fear is a powerful *negative* drive. It compels you forward while inhibiting your progress at the same time. Fear is like a noose that slowly tightens around your neck if you move in the wrong direction. Fear restricts your abilities and thoughts and leads you toward panic reactions. Even when you're standing on the threshold of success, your most creative and inventive plans can be sabotaged by fear.

> Hope is a magnet that draws you toward your goal.

Fear is also like a video continually replaying your most haunting experiences: moments of embarrassment, rejection, failure, hurt, and disappointment. The message of the fear video is clear: Life is full of these experiences, and they will repeat themselves. Fear causes you to say, "I can't do it; I may fail." You have a constant sense of living in the grip of fear.

Hope is a totally different motivating force—a *positive* drive. Hope is like a magnet that draws you toward your goal. Hope expands your life and brings a message of possibility and change. It draws you away from the bad experiences of the past and toward better experiences in the future. The hope video continually replays scenarios of potential success. Hope causes you to say, "I can do it; I will succeed." And it overrides "I don't feel safe."

What motivates you? What drives you? What pushes you ahead in life: fear or hope?

_____

_____

_____

_____

_____

OVERCOMING FEAR

Have you ever wondered why some people are able to overcome their fears while other people are overcome by their fears? Those who overcome their fears confront their fears head on in a realistic way.

Most fears need to be overcome gradually. Large or long-established fears are often too overwhelming to be conquered with one swift blow. Trying to conquer the fear immediately may actually cause the fear to grow instead of shrink. The best way to begin overcoming a fear is to face it a little at a time and from a safe distance.

As you begin to tame your fears, be realistic about your expectations. If you were to chart your improvement on a graph, don't expect to see a straight, upward line of uninterrupted success. Your growth and improvement will come in a series of ups and downs, and there will be times when your fears are actually worse. If you want to succeed in overcoming your fear, develop a strategy for doing so.

Specifically Identify What You Fear

Step 1: Take a sheet of paper and write down your fears.

Step 2: Once you have listed your specific fears, rank them in order of importance, beginning with whatever you fear the most.

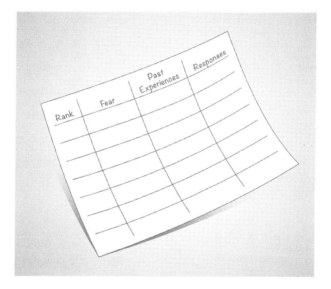

Step 3: Once you have identified and ranked your fears on a sheet of paper, write the heading "Past Experiences" Then describe two or three times when you actually experienced this fear. Use the most recent experiences you can remember, and give as many details as possible for these encounters.

Step 4: List all the symptoms (emotional responses, physical responses, and social responses) that you experienced the last time you met your fear face-to-face. Be as specific as possible when listing your reactions to these past fearful situations.

- Did you become immobilized or did you run?

- Did you try to remain calm and confront your fear, or did you scream and run away?

- What did you feel when you last confronted your fear? Did your heart beat faster?

- Did you perspire?

- Did you feel like fainting, or did your stomach begin to grind?

Build a Hierarchy

Building a hierarchy requires you to use your imagination in approaching the object, situation, or person you fear. You begin by imagining the least threatening situation in which you could involve yourself with this fear object. Gradually you move to the most threatening scenario. Each imaginary scene in between builds upon those previous to it.

Create a Self-Talk List

On the left side of a piece of paper, list some of the typical negative statements you make whenever you find yourself in the situation you fear. Then on the right side, list the statements you could make that will help you cope with the situation and face your fear.

What you say to yourself at this time may make the difference between overcoming your fear and continuing to be overcome by it. If your statements reflect negativism, you won't mature in your mastery over fear.

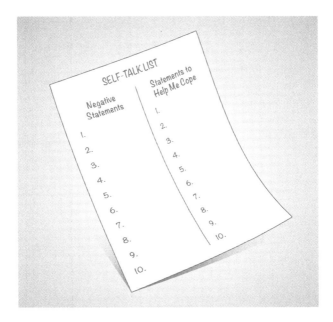

True, this exercise is a bit complex and involves a lot of effort. But for many, this process has been very effective. It is a step toward overcoming your fear. And your fears can be overcome—that's a promise from God!

Gregory Jantz suggests the following:

People often lament, "But what if" and use this unknown as a reason to continue living their lives paralyzed with fear. An effective way to move them past this stage is to see what life looks like at the other end of what-if. The way to do this is through the third step, to turn what-if into an if-what. For some fears, you may need to ask, "Okay, *if* this were to happen, *what* would it mean and *what* would I do?" (Again, depending on the nature of your fears and the level of your anxiety, consider working through this with a counselor or even a trusted friend or loved one.

Taming the monster of what-if sometimes takes the deeper examination of if-what. If the worst you can imagine were to happen, what would that mean? How would your life go on? What would you do? What would your life be like? You need to know there is life at the other end of your fears, even your greatest ones. You need to know you have resources and help available, even if the worst thing were to happen.[4]

GOD'S PLAN FOR OUR MIND

God does have a plan for our mind. He has an ideal for it. The New Testament describes or implies what a Christian's mind is to be like.

Our Mind Is to Be Alive

The Christian's mind is described in Romans 8:6 (NASB):

> *"For the mind set on the flesh is death, but the mind set on the Spirit is life and peace."*

When we invite Jesus Christ into our life, we have a new life. We come alive. We show this new life by the choices we make. It's a major adjustment for many. We're now faced with choices of what we think about, what we dwell on, what we put into our mind, what we say, and so on. I've heard some say, "After I invited Jesus into my life, I felt alive for the first time in my life."

Think about it. Take time to sit and reflect. Are you still struggling with the old thinking pattern, with clutter in your mind? Or is there a sense of being alive in your mind and thought life?

Fear and worries can be changed into feelings of rest and security. That's being alive.

Our Mind Is to Be Peaceful

You and I have choices as to what we focus on in our thought life. Paul said:

> "For those who are according to the flesh and are controlled by its unholy desires set their minds on and pursue those things which gratify the flesh, but those who are according to the Spirit and are controlled by the desires of the Spirit set their minds on and seek those things which gratify the [Holy] Spirit."
>
> — Romans 8:5, AMP

The very next verse tells us, "The mind of the [Holy] Spirit is life and [soul] peace" (v. 6, AMP). You and I *set* our minds. That's our work. The result of doing this is peace, which is God's work.

Our Mind Is to Stay Focused

> "But [now] I am fearful, lest that even as the
> serpent beguiled Eve by his cunning, so your
> minds may be corrupted and seduced from
> wholehearted and sincere and pure devotion
> to Christ."
>
> — 2 Corinthians 11:3, AMP

Distractions are all around us, and our thoughts can
drift and lead us astray. It takes effort to stay focused.

GOD'S PLAN FOR USEFUL FEARS

Some of our fears are useful to us, but most of them are useless. If our useless fears had only a brief life span, we could tolerate them. The problem is that useless fears tend to hang on for years; some even follow us to the grave. It's not the fear that bothers us; it's the consequences of fear.

A useful fear is one that prompts us to action in the face of a real threat. If I'm driving down the highway and a car traveling in the opposite direction swerves into my lane, the fear that strikes me is useful, because it prompts me to take evasive action.

A useful fear is an inner warning system.

If I feel pains in my chest, jaw, and left arm, the sudden fear of a heart attack is useful, because it drives me to seek immediate medical attention. If I'm strolling along a trail in Grand Teton National Park and come face-to-face with a six-hundred-pound bear, my momentary terror is useful, because it spurs me to put as much distance as possible between the bear and me. If I read in the newspaper that the savings bank in which I have deposited my money is about to fold, my fear is useful, because it encourages me to rescue my savings immediately.

A useful fear is an inner warning system alerting me that something is wrong in my life. A useful fear signals a real danger that must be confronted with corrective action. A lawyer once shared with me that when he was a student, he experienced a persistent, low-level fear of failing his bar exam. But this useful fear pushed him to study diligently for the exam, which he passed.

The Bible tells us that a reverential or respectful fear of God is a useful fear, because it leads to wisdom. Jesus Christ graphically described the useful fear of God:

"Do not be afraid of those who kill the body but cannot kill the soul. Rather, be afraid of the One who can destroy both soul and body in hell."
— Matthew 10:28

Hear the words of Jesus echoing throughout the New Testament and in our daily life: "Fear not . . . fear not . . . fear not . . . fear not."

We are never, never alone. We do not reach out by ourselves whether it be to another person or a group or a new venture in life. Jesus is with us. He does not isolate us from the hard times of life but plunges through them with us. The Old Testament abounds with the same words Jesus expressed:

> "Have you not known? Have you not heard? The everlasting God, the Lord, the Creator of the ends of the earth, does not faint or grow weary; there is no searching of His understanding. He gives power to the faint and weary, and to him who has no might He increases strength [causing it to multiply and making it abound]."
>
> — Isaiah 40:28-29, AMP

Fear not [there is nothing to fear], for I am with you; do not look around you in terror and be dismayed, for I am your God. I will strengthen and harden you to difficulties, yes, I will help you; yes, I will hold you up and retain you with My [victorious] right hand of rightness and justice."

— Isaiah 41:10, AMP

"When you pass through the waters I will be with you, and through the rivers, they shall not overwhelm you. When you walk through the fire, you shall not be burned or scorched, nor will the flame kindle upon you."

— Isaiah 43:2, AMP

Hear also the words of Paul in Romans 8:38–39 (AMP):

"For I am persuaded beyond doubt (am sure) that neither death nor life, nor angels nor principalities, nor things impending and threatening nor things to come, nor powers, nor

height nor depth, nor anything else in creation will be able to separate us from the love of God which is in Christ Jesus our Lord."

What do these verses say to us about our lives, our fears? During your most intense bout with fear, allow your mind to become an echo chamber resounding with the words of Jesus: "Fear not . . . fear not . . . fear not."

CHAPTER TWO

Worry

Worry. It knows no limits and has no boundaries.[5] The poor worry about getting money, and the wealthy worry about keeping it. Lewis Thomas, an American scientist and author, once wrote: "We are, perhaps, uniquely among the earth's creatures the worrying animal. We worry away our lives, fearing the future, discontent with the present, unable to take in the idea of dying, unable to sit still."[6] It doesn't matter what age you are—worry could be your constant companion, if you let it.

You've probably been in fog before. It's a misty moisture that puts a chill in the air and takes the curl out of your hair. Did you know, however, how much actual water is in fog? If there were a dense fog covering seven city blocks to a depth of 100 feet, the actual water content would be less than a glass of water. That's right: when it's condensed, all that fog, which slows traffic to a snail's pace and keeps you from seeing the building across the block, can fit into a drinking glass. The authors of *Helping Worriers* point out:

> Worry is like that. It clouds up reality. It chills us to the bone. It blocks the warmth and light of the sunshine. If we could see through the fog of worry and into the future, we would see our problems in their true light.[7]

What Is Worry?

How would you define worry? What sets it apart from anxiety or fear? When you experience anxiety, your body responds. Usually your muscles tighten and your heart races. Worry has been defined as the *thinking* part of anxiety, as a series of thoughts and images that are full of emotion—all negative. These thoughts are rarely uncontrollable, but they focus on something that has an uncertain outcome. The worrier is convinced beyond a shadow of a doubt that the outcome will be negative.

The word worry comes from an Anglo-Saxon root meaning "to strangle" or "to choke." Put your hands on your throat. Now squeeze. That's worry. Worry is the uneasy, suffocating feeling we often experience in times of fear, trouble, or problems. When we worry, we look pessimistically into the future and think of the worst possible outcomes to the situation of our life. Intense worry is about as useful to our thinking as lighted matches in a dynamite factory.

My family raises golden retrievers. We don't let them have bones to chew because they're not good for them. But have you ever seen a dog with a bone? We have a phrase for the way a dog becomes addicted to that bone: He "worries" it. He just gnaws and gnaws on it day and night. He won't let go and may growl at you if you try to take it away from him. He's looking for meat but usually finds gristle, bone and marrow. The dog buries his bone, then digs it up and gnaws on it again and even though it's covered with dirt and leaves. He'll bury it and repeat the process again and again. Worriers are the same: They bite and chew on their worry, bury it, dig it up, bury it and dig it up again.

Worry is thinking turned into poisoned thoughts.

WORRY: THE WAR WITHIN US

Worry is like a war that is raging inside us. Dr. John Haggai, founder of the Haggai Institute, describes the conflict this way:

> Worry divides the feelings; therefore the emotions lack stability. Worry divides the understanding; therefore convictions are shallow and changeable. Worry divides the faculty of perception; therefore observations are faulty and even false. Worry divides the faculty of judging therefore attitudes and decisions are often unjust. These decisions lead to damage and grief. Worry divides the determinative faculty; therefore plans and purposes. If not "scrapped" altogether, are not filled with persistence.[8]

Worry is thinking turned into poisoned thoughts. Worry has been described as a small trickle of fear that meanders through the mind until it cuts a channel into which all other thoughts are drained.

With worry there is dread of something just over the horizon. When you worry, you're preoccupied with something about yourself. And often you keep the worries to yourself. This tendency keeps you on edge. You're not fully relaxed.

In fact, worriers don't handle stress or upset as well as others. They're overly troubled by it. Worry has been called the fuel system for stress. When you worry, you add to your upset by coming up with several worst-case scenarios to your concern, but you're unable to know for sure which one is going to happen.

Worriers have a calling in life: They want to examine what can go wrong. They are like drivers on the freeway who come upon a grisly accident. It's horrible, but they have to look. Why? Because of fear and curiosity. Often, people know they could see something that they don't want to see, but they look anyway.

Dr. Gregory Jantz describes worry this way:

Worries are like weeds, they have a tendency to grow up overnight. One of worry's favorite, most-fertile soils is an over-busy life. An overcommitted, no-time-to-breathe daily pace produces a toxicity that poisons peace, calm, and contentment. On the other hand, worries thrive in this toxic environment. When you're so busy going from thing to thing, there's no time to stop, to evaluate, to determine your next course. There is no time for reflection. There is no time to take a breath and decide what to do next. When there's no time for you to decide, you've lost control.[9]

Worry is like a magnet that draws the worrier. Perhaps we're all interested in what can go wrong in our life. We're fascinated by the possibilities. And when a possibility is discovered, we latch onto it with all of our what-ifs.[10]

Worry is actually a kind of fear—a special kind. To create it, we elongate fear with two things—anticipation and memory. We then infuse it with our imagination and feed it with emotion. And then we have our creation.[11]

You've heard the word *catastrophe*? That's what worriers envision. In their mind they create the worst of all possible outcomes.[12] One of the best descriptions of worry I've found is from Dr. Gregory Jantz, founder of the Center for Counseling and Health Resources:

> Worry is the ultimate recycler. Any anxiety, fear, or concern is reused and recycled endlessly. Worry says if it happened once, it will happen again. Worry says just because it didn't happen doesn't mean it couldn't have. Worry says just because it didn't happen doesn't mean it won't. Worry says there's no guarantee about tomorrow unless it's a guarantee of disaster. Worry wants to heap up all the actual and perceived disasters of yesterday and pile them on today, as well as any possible problem of tomorrow. This is simply too heavy a load for today to bear; it will crush beneath the weight. Hope gets crushed, joy gets crushed, optimism gets crushed, as does any sense of perspective.[13]

PHYSICAL EFFECTS OF WORRY

Did you know that worry affects your sleep? Some worrying people tend to sleep on and on as though it's a rest from the drain of worry, but for most people worry is likely to create insomnia. The thoughts that race and tumble through your worry-filled mind interfere with your ability to relax and fall asleep.

There are other things that happen to your body when you worry. You may not be aware of them, but they are there. It takes an electroencephalogram (EEG) to show you. This test shows the brainwave differences that occur when people worry. When you worry excessively, your brain is even more heavily impacted. Worrying more and more about something (and I mean for hours a day, week after week) is like having a "switching station" in your brain get stuck. Remember when you have a cramp in a leg muscle and it stays and stays regardless of what you do? Well, worrying about something is like having a brain cramp that won't let go of your worry. The more you worry, the more you cut a groove in your brain and the more worry finds a home in which to reside. That's why other people's suggestions of "Don't worry" or "Just relax" won't work.[14]

What happens if you experience a major upset in your life? Then there is even more of a biological process that occurs. Your body goes into action, sending out various hormones and other substances in its response to the trauma. This actually makes the worry "burn" itself into the brain. It really becomes attached, and your brain's physical state changes. It can actually alter your brain's chemistry.[15]

WORRY AND ANXIETY

If fear and worry are first cousins, worry and anxiety have an even closer relationship. Worry and anxiety both refer to the inner turmoil we experience in fearful, stressful situations. The ancient Greeks described anxiety as opposing forces at work to tear a man apart.

We all worry; that's a given. But many worry excessively and thus end up suffering. Their worry is more than an annoyance; it actually hinders their lives.

There is a place in our lives for legitimate fear and concern, and at times a degree of anxiety when these are related to realistic situations. Not all anxiety is bad; it sometimes has a plus side. As Dr. O. Quentin Hyder suggests in *The Christian's Handbook of Psychiatry*:

A little [anxiety] in normal amounts can enhance performance. Athletes would be unable to perform successfully without. Businessmen do better in their competitive world than they could do without its stimulus. It definitely strengthens concentration and spurs imagination, thereby producing more creative ideas. It stimulates interest and develops ambition. It protects from danger.[16]

In its positive sense, anxiety is a God-given instinct that alerts us to fearful situations and prepares us to respond appropriately to them. But worry often takes a concern and makes it toxic. The *legitimate* responses form a built-in alarm system that works when needed, but worry is like a car alarm system that won't turn off and can drive the frustrated owner up a wall!

Pastor Earl Lee illustrates the difference:

Worry is like racing an automobile engine while it is in neutral. The gas and noise and smog do not get us anywhere. But legitimate concern . . . is putting the car into low gear on your way to moving ahead. You tell yourself that you are going to use the power God has given you to do something about the situation which could cause you to fret.[17]

Worry immobilizes you and does not lead to action, while legitimate concern moves you to overcome the problem.

There are many diseases in our world today, but worry is an old one—a disease of the imagination. It's like a virus that slowly and subtly overtakes and dominates your life. It's like an invading army that creeps ashore at night and eventually controls the country. When that happens, your ability to live life the way you want to is diminished. A Swedish proverb says, "Worry gives a small thing a big shadow."

Many Scripture verses describe the effects of worry and anxiety. And many other verses reveal that a worry-free life reaps many positive rewards. Notice the contrast in the verses that follow:

"Anxiety weighs down the heart."
— Proverbs 12:25

"A tranquil mind gives life to the flesh."
— Proverbs 14:30, RSV

"A glad heart makes a cheerful countenance,
but by sorrow of heart the spirit is broken."
— Proverbs 15:13, AMP

"All the days of the desponding and afflicted are made evil [by anxious thoughts and forebodings], but he who has a glad heart has a continual feast [regardless of circumstances]."

— Proverbs 15:15, AMP

"A happy heart is good medicine and a cheerful mind works healing, but a broken spirit dries the bones."

— Proverbs 17:22, AMP

WHY WE WORRY

What do we worry about?[18] It would be safe to say *everything*.

Dr. Samuel Kraines and Eloise Thetford suggest three categories into which most worries fall:

1. *Disturbing situations for which one must find a solution*—for example the basics such as how to obtain money for food, lodging or medical expenses.

2. *Disturbing situations over which one has no control*—for example, a mother dying of cancer, a usually prompt daughter who is five hours late, or a child in active combat.

3. *Unimportant, insignificant, minor problems of everyday life that warrant little attention, let alone "worry."* People "worry" about minor details of everyday life, concocting horrible possibilities and then "stewing" about them. [We worry that we're not doing well at work, that we will be fired,

and that we cannot pay our bills.] The list goes on and on. The worry is not only a feeling tone of fearfulness, but an overriding sense of futility, hopelessness and dreaded possibilities.[19]

Worrying intensely about the possibility of some event happening not only fails to prevent it from occurring but also can actually help to bring it about. Imagine a young seminary student waiting to preach his first sermon. He sits thinking about what he's going to say. He begins to worry about forgetting words, stumbling over certain phrases, and not presenting himself in a confident manner. As he continues to worry, he actually sees himself making these mistakes. And then when he gets up to preach, he makes the very mistakes he worried about! His worry became a self-fulfilling prophecy.

If you were to tell this student that he shouldn't have worried about his preaching, he probably would have replied, "I was justified in worrying. After all, those problems that I worried about were real problems. They happened, didn't they? I should have been worried." What he doesn't realize is that by his own worry, he actually helped the mistakes he worried about occur. He was responsible for his own failure. He spent more time seeing himself fail than he did visualizing himself succeeding or overcoming his fears.

The principle here is that if you spend time seeing yourself as a failure, you'll more than likely reproduce in your performance what you imagined. You actually condition yourself for negative performances because of your negative thinking. The classic example of this is the person who worries about getting an ulcer and in a few months is rewarded for his or her efforts with an ulcer. People who continually worry about having an accident on the freeway are very accident-prone. They are more likely to have accidents than other people because they constantly visualize such events.

However, if you spend the same amount of time and energy planning how to overcome your anticipated mistakes and envisioning your success as you do visualizing your failure, your performance will be far better.

The final results of fear, worry, and anxiety are negative, self-defeating, and incapacitating. What do we accomplish by worrying? Are there any positive results? Make a list of the things you worry about; then describe specifically what the worry has accomplished—or has it created more problems?

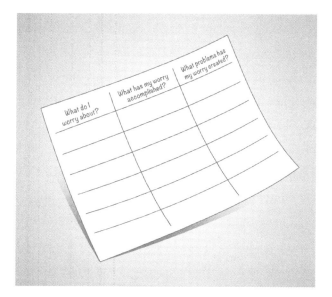

When you worry about a problem, real or imaginary, it usually keeps you from being able to do something effective about the problem. Worry, in other words, is a big problem in itself.

Do you enjoy worrying? Strong question? Worry seems to have a certain attraction in itself. Pain seems to grab our attention more readily than pleasure. Perhaps worrying is a bit like watching a scary horror movie: It's kind of exciting as well as entertaining. Or perhaps when you worry, you're getting some kind of stimulation. Your mind is engaged, locked in on a target like a heat-seeking missile.

Have you ever considered worry as a protective device? For some people it is. It's as though the worry portion of the brain has a spasm. It just can't seem to let go of the perceived problem and see the other side. Whatever the good news is, it's rejected.

Those who are depressed often turn to worry. If you have an obsessive-compulsive condition, worry can feel like the waves of an ocean. You can't seem to stop it. If you were traumatized, worry is your constant companion.

The Role of Physiology

Many individuals choose or learn to worry, but recently the role of physiology has been discovered to also be involved in worry. A study indicated that there is a gene that regulates one of the chemicals in our body called serotonin, which is believed to help maintain our feeling of wellbeing. Some people who have this gene may have an inclination to worry, and some people who have this gene actually look for an issue to worry about, since the only time they feel complete is when they do so.[20]

When we're born, we come into an inheritance. In fact it's been given to us prior to birth during the development process. It's as though we sit through the reading of a will and discover what our inheritance is going to be. Some of what we inherit makes life fuller and easier, while some has the opposite effect.

You may have inherited the tendency to be shy. Or you may have a nervous system and structure that are high-strung. Some people have a trigger mechanism for worry that is a hair trigger; the slightest touch sets it off. Some develop this over years of practice.

Technicians wire up computers, components, and other electronic instruments in certain ways; and we are all wired in unique ways as well. When we enter this life, we have a certain set of personality traits—or wiring, as it were. Some of us are wired to be extroverts and some of us to be introverts. Some of us are methodical and structured, while others can become lost between the front door and the car.

Dr. Edward Hallowell described our condition very well:

> Worries seem to inherit a neurological vulnerability that life events can then trigger. While some people are born confident, others are born insecure. While some people are born calm, others are born wired. While some people are born plunging forward, others are born holding back. You may be born with a specific characteristic or you may be born with a vulnerability to develop it later on, in the face of the stresses life usually presents.[21]

However, before any of us say, "That's it. That's the reason I worry: I can't help it. I'm genetically predisposed and predetermined to do so. Nothing I do will ever help, so why try?" consider these factors:

1. None of us knows for sure if that is the reason at this point.

2. This predisposition is also modified by our personality and life experiences. What we experience and learn in life can have an effect on how strongly a gene may be expressed, and (here is the big factor) *the expression of such a gene can be changed by experience and training.*[22]

Regardless of the reason we worry, we *can* learn to control its effect upon our lives. As Christians, we have the greatest opportunity to do so, because of the resources of our faith.

The Role of Genetics and Biochemistry

Anxiety was mentioned earlier, but let's look at it further to see how it differs from worry. Anxiety is a painful or apprehensive uneasiness of mind tied into some impending event. It's a response full of fear that impacts the body with responses that include sweating, muscles tensing, rapid pulse rate, and fast breathing. There is also a sense of doubt about both the reality of the threat and one's ability to handle it.

We all experience anxiety, but when it disrupts our lifestyle, we call it an *anxiety disorder*. Most anxiety is self-induced, but how does it develop? In fact, it tends to run in families. There appears to be some type of genetic bent toward this tendency, just like worry. Your environment also plays a role. This could include a family member who provided a role model of being a worrier, the expectation for you to be perfect, some form of abandonment as a child, and so on.

Anxiety can be influenced by biochemistry as well. Some of the personality traits that we develop can also contribute to an anxiety disorder, including the tendency to have huge expectations as well as to need the approval of everyone. When your mind dwells on these things, your biochemistry is affected, which can then make you more prone to being anxious. We call this the *adrenaline response*.

When you have an adrenaline response, a signal is sent to your brain, and an alarm system is activated. Your body then secretes a hormone called adrenaline. (That's just the beginning of the process). Your nervous system has been warned that something is wrong, that some danger may be present or possible. Then cortisol is secreted. These stimulants begin to flow through your body.

This biochemical response is *not* a malfunction of the central nervous system; it is a completely normal response. If a man wearing a ski mask were to burst into your home, your body would immediately respond by registering trouble. Then adrenaline and cortisol would start racing through your body. God created you with a central nervous system that is sensitive to the reception of these stimulants, and it reacts to them with the fight-

or-flight response. You are now ready to either defend yourself or run away as fast as you can. Your body is prepared for survival. This is a perfectly appropriate response from a healthy, functioning body preparing to protect itself. You're normal, and your body has gone into action. It's on call to protect you.[23]

Have you ever experienced getting "worked up" in your mind? You create a scenario in your thought life that is as real as life itself. Then your body responds as described above, as though you're confronted by the intruder in the ski mask:

> [Your] heart begins to pump faster, transporting oxygen to the muscles in your legs and arms. The stomach—a vulnerable center which in combat needs protection—contracts as blood moves swiftly away from it. You get a chronically upset stomach, nausea, or cramping and you think, *What if I have stomach cancer?* Blood rushes into the arms and legs and out of the hands and feet, the protruding limbs which are also vulnerable to being injured. Your fingers and toes become cold. They tingle

and you think, *What if I have multiple sclerosis?* Your heart pounds so hard, you think, *What if I'm having a heart attack?* The blood rushes out of your head causing dizziness and you think, *What if I have a brain tumor?* There is nothing to be done with your overstimulated system, so it turns in on itself. You are now just a step away from panic.[24]

Have you ever felt so anxious that you've been bewildered or even disoriented? You may have felt, *Oh no! I'm losing my mind! I'm going crazy!* You probably wanted to get rid of this bewildered feeling, because you thought it was bad. But actually that sort of feeling is a healthy response that helps you cope with the situation. If you struggle with excessive anxiety or any kind of phobias, you could experience these responses. This is your mind's way of taking a break or mini-vacation from your emotional overload.

Perfectionism is an exercise in frustration.

In a crisis or a trauma a person's normal system shuts down and a mild state of shock goes into action. The system needs to shut down because there is too much coming at the person for him or her to handle everything. The senses can't handle it all.

When you experience excessive anxiety the same thing happens. This is an adrenaline response. It won't hurt you and it will go away in a few hours. Instead of focusing on your anxiety, which will produce more adrenaline, tell yourself, *I'm all right; this is normal. God created my body to respond this way. This is protecting me from too much happening at once.*

The Role of Personality

Now let's consider some of the personality traits that can contribute to anxiety in our life.

Perfectionism is one culprit. I mentioned this before. Perfectionism is an impossibility. It's an exercise in frustration. I've never yet met a successful perfectionist. You can use the same energy to develop high standards and pursue excellence. If you're a perfectionist, you'll never be satisfied, but with excellence you can be. When you know you've done your best, you can gain a sense of enjoyment. Use your energy to work toward becoming comfortable with the fact that things aren't perfect and never will be.

Another culprit is how you interpret the feelings you have inside. Perhaps you decide to go river rafting. As you approach the rapids and see the water churning and frothing, your heart pounds, your hands sweat, and you have difficulty breathing. What do you say to yourself? You could say to yourself, *I'm terrified. I'm going to drown. They'll never find my body.* You'll fill with fear. You'll feel panicky.

Or you could say, *This is wild. It's so exciting. What a trip! It's okay for my heart to pound and my palms to be this sweaty.* By thinking this, you'll feel *excitement* rather than fear.

The OCD Syndrome

One of the most intense expressions of worry is OCD—obsessive-compulsive disorder. For someone with this disorder, worry seems to rule the mind like a tyrant! Certain thoughts come into the person's mind and they can't be evicted. The person affected with OCD has a variety of intense, unwanted thoughts that he or she is obsessed with. Sometimes the person feels compelled to do certain rituals that are supposed to keep specific consequences from occurring. It could be turning off the faucet a certain way five times, closing all the doors, lining up the papers on a desk to match perfectly, or having all the cans spaced perfectly in the cupboards—to name just a few examples.

Between 1 and 3 percent of our population experience this syndrome. In a way OCD is an intensification of the fears and worries that most people experience, but for a person with OCD, these fears dominate his or her life. One of the best descriptions of this disorder was written by Judith Rapopport in her book *The Boy Who Couldn't Stop Washing*.[25] Fortunately, there are various treatments available today for this disorder.[26] (If you are experiencing OCD, it would be beneficial to talk with a professional counselor.)

Part of the solution is to first learn as much as you can about worry and anxiety. Don't run from it, and don't believe that it cannot be overcome. It can.

Sometimes it helps to *take action* rather than give in to the worry. If what you are worrying about needs some action, then take some action. Immobility feeds worry just as it feeds depression.

Perhaps you've seen films of the inside of a cockpit of a fighter plane. Most of our military planes rely upon missiles for their weaponry. In front of the pilot is a screen that shows the enemy plane. The pilot guides the flight of his or her plane in order to line it up for the missile. When the fighter is correctly lined up, the screen lights up with a "missile lock" message. The missile is locked onto that enemy plane until it's destroyed.

In the same way, worry seems to lock onto a problem and won't let go. Then it sends an alarm signal to the front part of the brain, which analyzes the worry. The front portion sends a signal back to the worry, which says, "I'm worrying now." The worry then becomes alarmed even more and sends a signal back to the front, and thus it goes on and on. It's like a circuit that can't be broken. It's as though the worry has taken control of the brain and shuts out the rest of life around you.

Positive and Negative "What ifs"

Here is a simple way to tackle the "what ifs" of worry and anxiety: Just take every anxious "what if" and turn it around to make it positive. Here are some examples:

Negative: What if I never get over my worry?
Positive: What if I do overcome my worry?

Negative: What if I forget what I'm supposed to say?
Positive: What if I remember everything I want to say?

Negative: What if I mess up and lose my job?
Positive: What if I do all right and keep my job?

Negative: What if I never get off my medication?
Positive: What if I get off my medication?

Negative: What if the new people don't like me?
Positive: What if the new people really like me?

Negative: What if I fail the test?
Positive: What if I pass the test and do very well?

The negative way of thinking creates more worry and anxiety; the positive way creates anticipation, excitement, and hope. Practice turning your negative "what ifs" into positive statements:

Negative: What if _____

_____

Positive: What if _____

_____

Negative: What if _____

_____

Positive: What if _____

_____

Negative: What if _____

_____

Positive: What if _____

_____

Negative: What if _____

_____

Positive: What if _____

_____

The Principle of Replacement

Another way to handle your anxiety is to *counter* your
negative thoughts. This is known as the principle
of replacement. Yes, it will take time, effort, and
repetition, but it will be effective.

The following are some examples of typical
negative thoughts and some suggestions on how you
can challenge them and shift them to positive thoughts:

Negative: When will I get over these panic feelings? I feel so afraid sometimes, and this drains my energy.

Positive: I'm working on overcoming these panic attacks. Will these hurt me? No. I'll just let these feelings come when they want to, and eventually they'll go away.

Negative: I feel as if my anxious feelings are controlling my life. I hate this situation. I feel stuck.

Positive: So . . . it's just anxiety. It's no big deal. Anxiety is a part of life. I'm doing better. I'm learning to control it. I'm better this week than I was last week. It will take time, but I will conquer it with the Lord's help.

Negative: I don't want to go anywhere today. What if I get sick?

Positive: It's okay to feel these feelings. I haven't gone anywhere for a long time. I'm not going to be sick. I'm okay. I'll be just fine. I'll focus on how I can enjoy this outing. It's never as bad as I anticipate it to be.

Negative: Sometimes I feel like I'm never going to get control of my anxiety and worry. It's like a deeply ingrained habit!

Positive: Look how I've grown already by being able to identify the pattern. Imagine where I'll be in six weeks or months! I'm doing well. I can thank God for the changes that have occurred in my life.

Negative: Why is that person so mad at me? Did I do something? Is it something I said?

Positive: I'm taking this much too seriously. I'm not a mind reader. How do I know he's mad at me? I don't. If he's mad, it's his concern, not mine. It's up to him to tell me if it's me.

Negative: What if I try the new job and I don't like it or don't do well? I'd feel so upset.

Positive: Trying is an accomplishment! If it doesn't work out, at least I took the chance. That in itself is a new and positive step.

Negative: These anxious feelings make me feel like I'm losing my mind. They're so unpleasant.

Positive: I know what these feelings cause. I know I'm emotional and I didn't eat right. It isn't worth getting anxious about it. I'll feel better in the future.[27]

Challenge your own negative thoughts below:

Negative: _____

_____

_____

Positive: _____

_____

_____

Negative: _____

_____

_____

Positive: _____

_____

_____

Negative: _____

_____

_____

Positive: _____

_____

_____

Negative: _____

_____

_____

Positive: _____

_____

_____

Face Your Worry and Anxiety Head-on

One of the ways to deal with intense worries or anxiety is to face them head-on. The more we run from them, the larger they grow. The best way to deal with them is to face them directly. In baseball there is a guideline that infielders follow: Play the ground ball; don't let the ground ball play you. The point is that in order to field a ground ball cleanly, there's one step to follow: Instead of backing up and trying to predict the bounces as the ball comes to you, do just the opposite. *Charge the ball*, and in doing this you'll act rather than think too much. You'll grab the ball before you have a chance to think yourself into making an error. (You don't want to be at the mercy of the unpredictable bounces the ball makes. This is called letting the ball play you.) How can you apply this to a worry or anxiety you have? When a worry or fear arises, don't try to avoid the thought.

The more we run from our worries, the larger they grow.

Welcome it and take control of its presence. You could say to yourself, *Well, here you are again. You're a pain. I don't like you, but I've dealt with you before. But this time it's not just you and I. It's you and I and my Lord Jesus. I'm giving you to him, and he will give me the peace I desire to banish you.*

Take Little Steps

If you really are afraid of something, try exposing yourself to it a little bit at a time, until you're comfortable with it. Years ago a woman came to see me who was deathly afraid of earthquakes. Now that's one of the four "seasons" we have in Southern California—earthquakes. They're kind of hard to avoid! She had been through the destructive Sylmar earthquake in the early 1970s and was traumatized by it. She worried every day that she would go through another one. She was so worried that for the past ten years she had avoided reading newspapers and listening to or watching any news programs in order to avoid hearing about any earthquakes. This did nothing but intensify her fears.

Finally she realized that this was no way to live, so she came for help. We worked together for several months. Each week we talked a bit more about earthquakes. She learned to face them, rather than run from them. She graduated from counseling after she went to the library, checked out a book on earthquakes and read it. She realized that she will experience more of these in her lifetime and will have to deal with each one when it comes. But for now, she didn't need to worry about the next one. She faced her fear slowly and consistently, and gradually she broke the hold it had on her.

Evaluate, Plan, and Remediate

Dr. Edward Hallowell has developed an approach called EPR: evaluate, plan, and remediate.[28] If this becomes a habit, it can defeat the onslaught of many of your worries, because it's an approach that turns worry into action. It's a form of plan-making. I know that some personality types aren't really into plan-making, but regardless of who we are, we can and perhaps need to do this to bring more order into our life.

Perhaps you've had some shooting pains in your lower back that come and go. One day they're there; the next day they're not. But the pattern persists for several weeks. You read a couple of articles that appear to describe the symptoms that you are having, but the outcome for the individual described was terminal cancer. After reading this, your mind takes over, because the seeds of worry were planted. Then the worry intensifies. Instead of creating misery, you could do the following:

Evaluate: Say to yourself: *This is a new condition for me. The pain is not overwhelming but annoying. I don't like the pattern it's developing. It doesn't seem to be going away on its own.*

Plan: Say to yourself: *I don't know the causes or what this means. I know I avoid doctors, but the persistence of this means I need to talk to a doctor.*

Remediate: You call your doctor and make an appointment.

It sounds so simple, it's almost insulting. You may be thinking: *That's just what I do all the time!* Great, but many worriers become immobilized and never even get to the first phase, evaluate.

Here's another one: Suppose you've been asked to host a meeting at your home in two days. Without thinking about what may need to be done around your house, you agreed to the meeting. Just thinking about all that has to be done, however, as well as wanting to make a good impression, your body begins to tense up and worry begins to run through your mind. You start one task, become distracted, and then go to another. Nothing is getting done, except that you're getting more and more upset. Instead of continuing to get upset, you could do the following:

> *Evaluate:* Say to yourself: *It's true. I've got a problem. I've been letting the house go and it is a mess. It's cluttered, and the way I'm trying to solve this isn't working. I've got to do something better than what I'm doing now.*

Plan: Say to yourself: *All right, the people will probably be in just three rooms—the living room, bathroom, and kitchen. I'll concentrate on those three to clean and declutter. I'll stay in one room and one section of that room and stay until it's done. That way I can see progress.*

Remediate: You tackle the largest room first and complete it.

Constructive Concern

Did you ever consider the idea that a form of worry could be productive? I like to call it the CC process, or constructive concern. Actually it's a preventive to worry and anxiety. Andrew Grove, the successful CEO of Intel, a very successful company, wrote *Only the Paranoid Survive: How to Exploit the Crisis Points That Challenge Every Company*. It's a book that invites people to succeed. Grove suggests that instead of not being paranoid, being *creatively* paranoid is the way to succeed. He suggests that we anticipate every possible alternative, learn from it, and do something about it.

So instead of ignoring your real or possible problems, you should be positive about your ability to deal with the negative.[29]

Inventory Your Worries

Whenever worry plagues you, use some or all of the following suggestions to help you inventory your worries and plan your strategy:

1. Be sure to have your doctor give you a complete physical examination. Have him or her check your glands; check for vitamin deficiencies, allergies, and fatigue; and go over your exercise schedule,

2. Face your worries and admit them when they occur. Don't run from them, for they will return to haunt you. Do not worry about worrying. That just reinforces and perpetuates the problem.

3. Itemize your worries and anxieties on a sheet of paper. Be specific and complete as you describe them.

4. Write down the reasons or causes for your worry. Investigate the sources. Is there any possibility that you can eliminate the source of the cause of your worry? Have you tried? What have you tried specifically?

5. Write down the amount of time you spend each day worrying.

6. What has worrying accomplished in your life? Describe the benefits in detail.

7. Make a list of the following: (a) the ways your worrying has prevented a feared situation from occurring; (b) the ways your worrying increased the problem.

8. If you are nervous or jumpy, try to eliminate the possible sources or irritation. Stay away from them until you learn how to react differently. For example, if troubling world events worry you, don't watch so many newscasts. Use that time to relax by reading, working in the garden, or riding a bike for

several miles. Avoid rushing yourself. If you worry about being late, plan to arrive at a destination early. Give yourself more time.

9. Avoid any type of fatigue—physical, emotional, or intellectual. When you are fatigued, worrisome difficulties can loom out of proportion.

10. When you do get involved in worry, is it over something that really pertains to you and your life, or does it properly belong to someone else? Remember that your fears or worries often may be disguised fears of what others think.

11. When a problem arises, face it and decide what you can do about it. Make a list of all the possible solutions and decide which you think is the best one. If these are minor decisions, make them fairly quickly. Take more time for major decisions.

A worrier usually says, "I go over and over these solutions and cannot decide which is best." Look at the facts; then make yourself decide. Or ask yourself, *If a friend of mine was looking at these possibilities, which would I recommend he choose and why?* After you have made your decision, do not question or worry about your choice. Otherwise the worrying pattern erupts all over again. Practice the new pattern of making decisions.

Exercise

Exercise is one of the best anti-worry responses you can use. (As long as you don't continue to worry while you are exercising!) Did you know that exercise works as an antidepressant, reduces tension, reduces frustration and anger, improves your sleep, helps your concentration, and helps keep you from being distracted? It can help improve your weight, blood pressure, and heart rate. Over the past 15 years of regular exercise, my resting heart rate went from 80 to 58. While you exercise, you can memorize Scripture, read (if you're riding a stationary bike), or pray.

Consult a Specialist

Sometimes worry or anxiety is so intense that for a while medication is a helpful solution. It can help the anxious or worried brain put on the brakes. Medication is not a cure-all but is simply one of the several forms of treatment. It should be used only when indicated, and only a physician should be the one to prescribe it (sometimes in conjunction with a counselor or a therapist).

CHAPTER THREE

Biblical Answers

Anxiety may stem from unconscious feelings, but worry is a conscious act of choosing an ineffective method of coping with life. According to Oswald Chambers, the great evangelist and author, all our fret and worry is caused by calculating without God. Here's the big question: Does worry have any place in the life of the Christian?[30] Is it a sin to worry or to feel anxiety?

As we've discussed, people who experience extreme states of anxiety may not be able to control them. They may feel that they are at the mercy of their feelings, because they can't pin down exactly why they're so anxious. Such individuals may have deep, hidden feelings or hurts that have lingered for years in the subconscious. In such cases, perhaps they need to face their problems, discover the roots of their feelings, and replace them with the healing power and resources offered through Jesus Christ and Scripture.

But freedom from worry *is possible*. The answer lies in tapping the resources of Scripture. Read each passage cited below before reading the paragraphs that follow it.

WORRY DOESN'T WORK, SO DON'T DO IT

Matthew 6:25–34

From this passage we can discover several principles to help us overcome anxiety and worry. First, note that Jesus did not say, "Stop worrying when everything is going all right for you." His command is not a suggestion. He simply and directly said to stop worrying about your life. In a way, Jesus was saying we should learn to accept situations that can't be altered at the present time. That doesn't mean we're to sit back and make no attempt to improve conditions around us. But we must face tough situations without worry and must learn to live with them while we work toward improvement.

Second, Jesus said you can't add any length of time to your life by worrying. Not only is this true, but the reverse is also true: The physical effects of worry can actually shorten your life span.

Third, the object of your worry may be a part of the difficulty. It could be that your sense of values is distorted and that what you worry about should not be the center of your attention. The material items that seem so important to you should be secondary to spiritual values.

Fourth, Christ also tells you to live a day at a time. You may be able to change some of the results of past behavior, but you cannot change some of the results of past behavior and you can't predict or completely prepare for the future, so don't inhibit its potential by worrying about it. Focus your energies on the opportunities of today!

Most of the future events that people worry about don't happen anyway. Furthermore, the worrisome anticipation of certain inevitable events is usually more distressing than the actual experience itself. Anticipation is the magnifying glass of our emotions. And even if an event is as serious as we may anticipate, we as Christians can look forward to God's supply of strength and stability at all times.

FOCUS ON THE SOLUTION, NOT THE PROBLEM

Matthew 14:22–33

In this passage, we find the disciples in a boat as Jesus walked toward them on the water. When Peter began to walk toward Jesus on the water, he was fine until his attention was drawn away from Jesus to the storm. Then he became afraid and started to sink.

If Peter had kept his attention upon Christ (the source of his strength and the solution to his problem), he would have been all right. But when he focused upon the wind and the waves (the problem and the negative aspect of his circumstances), he became overwhelmed by the problem, even though he could have made it safely to Jesus.

Fear and worry are like that. We focus so hard on the problem that we take our eyes off the solution and thus create more difficulties of ourselves.

We can be sustained in the midst of any difficulty by focusing our attention on the Lord and relying upon him:

> "Blessed is the man who trusts in the LORD, whose confidence is in him. They will be like a tree planted by the water that sends out its roots by the stream. It does not fear when heat comes; its leaves are always green. It has no worries in a year of drought and never fails to bear fruit.
>
> The heart is deceitful above all things and beyond cure. Who can understand it?

I the Lord search the heart and examine the
mind, to reward each person according to their
conduct, according to what their deeds deserve."
— Jeremiah 17:7–10

MAKE A CHOICE NOT TO WORRY

Luke 21:14–15

"Make up your mind not to worry beforehand
how you will defend yourselves. For I will
give you words and wisdom that none of your
adversaries will be able to resist or contradict."

At the beginning of the verses from Luke is a phrase that is a command, but one that also implies that we have the capability of doing it. "Make up your mind" means we have a choice as to whether *we choose* to worry or *choose not* to worry. "Make up your mind" is translated from a Greek word that means "to premeditate." You've probably heard this word used in criminal trials. If someone is accused of a premeditated crime, it means the accused thought through the crime beforehand. Choosing not to worry will take more effort and energy for some people than others, but change is possible.

You and I live in an unstable world. Sometimes the stock market seems to drop several hundred points for no reason. This creates not only worry but also fear, anxiety, and panic in some people. But when we trust in the Lord (and not the stock market), we receive the blessing of stability in a fragmented world. We have the ability to be free from worry in a world where there is much to be anxious and fearful about.

GIVE GOD YOUR WORRY IN ADVANCE

1 Peter 5:7

Peter must have learned from his experience of walking on the water, because he later wrote: "Cast all your anxiety on [God] because he cares for you." *Cast* means "to give up" or "to unload." The tense of the verb here refers to a direct once-and-for-all committal to God of all anxiety or worry. We are to unload on God our tendency to worry, so that when problems arise, we will not worry about them. We can cast our worry on God with confidence, because he cares for us. He is not out to break us down but to strengthen us and to help us stand firm. He knows our limits, and "a bruised reed he will not break, and a dimly burning wick he will not quench" (Isaiah 42:3, RSV).

Isaiah rejoiced to the Lord, "You will guard him and keep him in perfect and constant peace whose mind [both its inclination and its character] is stayed on You" (AMP). Whatever you choose to think about will either produce or dismiss feelings of anxiety and worry. Those people who suffer from fear and worry are choosing to center their minds on negative thoughts in this way. God has made the provision, but *you must take the action.* Freedom from fear and worry and anxiety is available, but you must lay hold of it. Center your thoughts on God, not on worry.

REPLACE FRETTING WITH TRUST

Psalm 37:1–40

Psalm 37 begins "Do not fret," and those words are repeated later in the psalm. The dictionary defines *fret* as "to eat away, gnaw, gall, vex, worry, agitate, wear away."

Whenever I hear the word *gnaw*, I'm reminded of a scene I see each year when I hike along the Snake River in the Grand Teton National Park in Wyoming where colonies of beavers live along the riverbanks. Often I see trees at various stages of being gnawed to the ground by them. Other trees have several inches of bark eaten away, and some have already fallen on the ground, because the beavers have gnawed through the trunks. Worry has the same effect on us: It will gradually eat away at us until it destroys us.

In addition to telling us not to fret, Psalm 37:1–7 gives us positive substitutes for fear and worry. First, it says, "Trust (lean on, rely on, and be confident) in the Lord" (verse 3 AMP). Trust is a matter of not attempting to live an independent life or to cope with difficulties alone. It means going to a greater source for strength.

Second, verse 4 says, "Delight yourself also in the Lord" (AMP). *To delight* means to rejoice in God and what he has done for us, to let God supply the joy for our life.

Third, verse 5 says, "Commit your way to the Lord" (AMP). Commitment is a definite act of the will, and it involves releasing our fears and worries and anxieties to the Lord.

And fourth, we are to "rest in the Lord; wait for Him" (verse 7, AMP). This means to submit in silence to what he ordains, and to be ready and expectant for what he is going to do in our life.

STOP WORRYING AND START PRAYING

Philippians 4:6–9

The passage in Philippians can be divided into three basic stages. We are given a *premise*: Stop worrying. We are given a *practice*: Start praying. And we are given a *promise*: Peace. The promise is there and available, but we must follow the first two steps in order for the third to occur. We must stop worrying and start praying if we are to begin receiving God's peace.

Psalm 34:1–4

The results of prayer as a substitute for fear and worry can be vividly seen in a crisis in David's life that prompted him to write Psalm 34 (see also 1 Samuel 21:10–22:2). David had escaped death at the hands of the Philistines by pretending to be insane. He then fled to the cave of Adullam, along with 400 men who were described as distressed and discontented and in debt. In the midst of all this, David wrote a psalm of praise that begins: "I will bless the Lord at all times; his praise shall continually be in my mouth" (Psalm 34:1, RSV). David did not say he would praise the Lord *sometimes but at all times*, even when his enemies were after him.

How could David bless the Lord in the midst of his life-threatening experience? Because he stopped worrying and started praying: "I sought the Lord, and he answered me, and delivered me from all my fears" (verse 4, RSV). David didn't turn around and take his cares back after he had deposited them with the Lord. He gave them up. Too many people give their burdens to God with a rubber band attached. As soon as they stop praying, the problems bounce back. They pray, "Give us this day our daily bread," and as soon as they are through praying, they begin to worry where their next meal is going to come from.

Another factor to notice is that God did not take David away from his problem in order to deliver him from his fears. When he wrote the Psalm 34, David was still hiding in the cave with 400 disgruntled men. God does not always take us out of problematic situations, but He gives us the peace we seek as we proceed prayerfully through each experience. It happened to David, and it happens today to those who pray, unload their cares on God, and leave them there.

REMEMBER THAT GOD IS WITH YOU

Isaiah 41:10

"Do not fear, for I am with you; do not be dismayed, for I am your God. I will strengthen you and help you; I will uphold you with my righteous right hand."

Through Isaiah, God tells us not to fear, and then he tells us why: "For I am with you." There is no better reason to stop being fearful or worried than the one given here: God is with you. *Dismayed* here means "to gaze," to look around in an anxious way. This word is used to describe a person who is looking around in amazement or bewilderment. It conveys the idea of being immobilized or paralyzed. You can't make up your mind which way to turn.

But once again there is a solution: God says, "I am your God." He is with us not eight hours a day, not twelve or sixteen, but twenty-four hours each day. When he says "I will strengthen you," he means he will make us be alert or be fortified with courage. When he says he will "help you," the word *help* is used to mean "summon." Imagine yourself surrounded by the loving arms of God. In fact each time you worry, say to yourself: *I am surrounded by the loving arms of God*, and see whether your fear or worry wants to stick around.

The words "I will uphold you" in verse 10 mean that God will sustain us. In music, when the conductor tells singers "Sustain that note," they keep singing it on and on until they've exhausted their air supply. But there is no exhaustion on God's part in sustaining us.[31]

BREAK THE PATTERN

Again and again the Scriptures give us the answer for fears and worries, but do you know *how* to break the fear and worry pattern in your own life? I'm talking about practical strategies by which you can apply the guidelines of Scripture to your specific worries. Let me share with you a few tips that others have used successfully over the years.

Make a Value Judgment

Let me illustrate this first suggestion for breaking the pattern by taking you into my counseling office. I was working with a man who had a roaring tendency to worry. We had talked through the reasons for his worry, and he had tried some of my suggestions for conquering his problem. But it seemed to me he was resistant to giving up his worry. (This isn't unusual; many people have worried for so long that they have grown comfortable with their negative patterns of thinking. It's actually all they know. They're successful with it and are unsure they will be successful with the new style of thinking.)

So one day I gave him an assignment that really caught him off guard: "It appears that worry is an integral part of your life and that you are determined to keep this tendency. But you only worry periodically throughout the day, with no real plan for worrying. So let's set up a definite worry time for you each day, instead of spreading it out.

"Tomorrow when you begin to worry about something, instead of worrying at that moment, write down what you're worried about on an index card and keep the card in your pocket. Each time a worry pops up, write it on the card, but don't worry about it yet. Then about 4:00 pm, go into a room where you can be alone. Sit down, take out the card, and worry about the items as intensely as you can for thirty minutes. Start the next day with a new blank card and do the same thing. What do you think about that idea?"

He stared at me in silence for several moments. "That's got to be one of the dumbest suggestions I've ever heard," he finally answered. "I can't believe I'm paying you to hear advice like that."

I smiled and said, "Is it really much different from what you're doing already? Your behavior tells me you like to worry, so I'm just suggesting you put it into a different time frame." As he thought about my comment, he realized I was right: He really wanted to worry. And until he decided he didn't want to worry, there was nothing I could do to help him.

This is very important: *Unless you make a value judgment on your negative behavior, you will never change.*

The issue parallels the question Jesus asked the lame man at the pool of Bethesda:

> *"Do you want to become well? [Are you really in earnest about getting well]?"*
>
> — John 5:6, AMP

You must make some conscious, honest decisions about your fear or worry. Do you like it or dislike it? Is it to your advantage or disadvantage? Is your life better with it or without it? If you're not sure, apply the techniques in this chapter and commit yourself not to worry for a period of just two weeks. Then, from your own experience, decide whether you prefer a life of worry or a life of freedom from worry.

Tell Yourself to Stop

During one session of a Sunday school class I was teaching on the subject of worry, I asked the participants to report on an exercise I had suggested the previous week for kicking the worry out of their lives. One woman said she began the experiment Monday morning, and by Friday she felt the worry pattern that had plagued her for years was finally broken.

What accomplished this radical improvement? It was a simple method of applying God's Word to her life in a new way. I have shared this method with hundreds of people in my counseling office and with thousands in classes and seminars.

Take a blank index card and on one side write the word *STOP* in large, bold letters. On the other side write the complete text of Philippians 4:6–9. (I especially like the *Amplified Bible* translation that follows. No matter which translation you use, it's interesting to note that Paul says that *God* will guard our heart, but *we* are to guard our mind.) Keep the card with you at all times. Whenever you're alone and begin to worry, take the card out, hold the stop side in front of you, and say aloud "Stop!" twice with emphasis. Then turn the card over and read the Scripture passage aloud twice with emphasis.

"Do not fret or have any anxiety about anything, but in every circumstance and in everything, by prayer and petition (definite requests), with thanksgiving, continue to make your wants known to God. And God's peace [shall be yours, that tranquil state of a soul assured of its salvation through Christ, and so fearing nothing from God and being content with its earthly lot of whatever sort that is, that peace] which transcends all understanding shall garrison and mount guard over your hearts and minds in Christ Jesus. For the rest, brethren, whatever is true, whatever is worthy of reverence and is honorable and seemly, whatever is just, whatever is pure, whatever is lovely and lovable, whatever is kind and winsome and gracious, if there is any virtue and excellence, if there is anything worthy of praise, think on and weigh and take account of these things [fix your minds on them]. Practice what you have learned and received and heard and seen in me, and model your way of living on it, and the God of peace (of untroubled, undisturbed well-being) will be with you." (AMP)

Taking the card out interrupts your thought pattern of fear and worry. Saying "Stop!" further breaks your automatic habit pattern of worry. Then reading the Word of God aloud becomes the positive substitute for worry. If you are in a group of people and begin to worry, follow the same procedure, only do it silently.

The woman who shared with the class her experience with this method said that on the first day of her experiment, she took out the card twenty times during the day. But on Friday she took it out only three times. She said, "For the first time in my life, I have the hope that my worrisome thinking can be chased out of my life."

Freedom from worry is possible! It requires that you practice the diligent application of God's Word in your life. This means repetitive behavior. If you fail the first time, don't give up. You may have practiced fear and worry for many years, and now you need to practice consistently the application of Scripture over a long period in order to completely establish a new, fear- and worry-free pattern.

Notes

1   Much of this chapter is from H. Norman Wright, *Finding Freedom from Your Fears* (Ada, MI: Revell, 2005).

2   John Haggai, *How to Win over Worry: A Practical Formula for Successful Living* (Eugene, OR: Harvest House, 1987), p. 73.

3   H. Norman Wright, *Overcoming Your Hidden Fears* (Wheaton, IL: Scripture Press, 1985), adapted.

4   Gregory L. Jantz with Ann McMurray, *Overcoming Anxiety, Worry and Fear: Practical Ways to Find Peace* (Grand Rapids, MI: Revell, 2011), p. 125.

5   Much of this chapter is from H. Norman Wright, *Winning over Your Emotions* (Eugene, OR: Harvest House Publishers, 2012), chapter 1.

6   Lewis Thomas, *The Medusa and the Snail: More Notes of a Biology Watcher* (New York: Penguin Books, 1995), p. 17.

7   James R. Beck and David T. Moore, *Helping Worriers: A Short-Term Structured Model* (Grand Rapids: Baker Books 1994), p. 26.

8   Haggai, *How to Win over Worry*, pp. 16–17.

9   Jantz, *Overcoming Anxiety, Worry, and Fear*, p. 175.

10 Edward M. Hallowell, *Worry* (New York: Ballantine Books, 1997), pp. 73–74.

11 Ibid., p. 9.

12 Beck and Moore, *Helping Worriers*, pp. 31–33.

13 Jantz, *Overcoming Anxiety, Worry, and Fear*, p. 179.

14 Hallowell, *Worry*, p. 5.

15 Ibid.

16 O. Quentin Hyder, *The Christian's Handbook of Psychiatry* (Old Tappan, NJ: Fleming H. Revell, 1971).

17 Earl Lee, *Recycled for Living* (Ventura, CA: Regal Books, 1973), p. 4.

18 Much of this section is from Wright, *Winning over Your Emotions*, chapter 2.

19 Samuel H. Kraines and Eloise S. Thetford, *Help for the Depressed* (Springfield, IL: Charles C. Thomas, 1979), pp. 190–91.

20 Hallowell, *Worry*, p. 61.

21 Ibid., p. 67.

22 Ibid., pp. 56–65.

23 Lucinda Bassett, *From Panic to Power: Proven Techniques to Calm Your Anxieties, Conquer Your Fears, and Put You in Control of Your Life* (New York: Harper Collins, 1995), pp. 32–33.

24 Ibid., p. 33.

25 Judith L. Rapopport, *The Boy Who Couldn't Stop Washing: The Experience and Treatment of Obsessive-Compulsive Disorder* (New York: New American Library, 1991).

26 For an in-depth look at this problem, see Gail Steketee and Kevin White, *When Once Is Not Enough: Help for Obsessive-Compulsives* (Oakland, CA: New Harbinger Publications, 1990).

27 Lucinda Bassett, *From Power to Panic* (New York: HarperCollins, 1997), adapted, pp. 156–57.

28 Hallowell, *Worry*, p. 242.

29 Ibid., pp. 38–39.

30 Much of this section is from H. Norman Wright, *Winning over Your Emotions* (Eugene, OR: Harvest House Publishers, 2012), chapter 3.

31 Beck and Moore, *Helping Worriers*, pp. 19–20.

Other titles by Dr. Norm Wright

Discovering Who You Are and How God Sees You

When we know who we are in God's eyes, our confidence won't allow the ups and downs of life destroy our self-worth. Releasing our dependence on having the right job, the right posessions, and hanging out with the right people will bring us a deeper sense of peace and satisfaction that no disappointment can take away.
ISBN 9781628620504

Helping Your Hurting Teen

Is your teen withdrawing, acting unusual, sullen or distracted? Do you feel like you just don't know your child anymore? Are you afraid it's more than just a stage? Learn which responses are "normal" adolescent behaviors, and which ones indicate deeper issues related to loss or trauma. Expert Dr. Norm Wright gives insight on how to reconnect with your child, understand their struggle, and never lose hope. **ISBN 9781628620542**

Recovering from the Loss of a Love

How do you cope when someone you love walks away from you? Whether it is the agony of unrequited love or the loss of a breakup, this book helps you move through the stages of grief and loss, and guides you toward wholeness and hope. Author Dr. Norm Wright compassionately and practically helps you work through the feeling of loss, grief, and rejection.
ISBN 9781628620580